A

TREATISE

ON THE CORRUPTION OF A
CONSTITUTIONAL
GOVERNMENT

www.northsouthpublishing.com

First Edition 2016

Manufactured in the United States of America by North South Publishing.

Printed in Charleston, South Carolina

For information regarding special discounts on bulk purchases, please contact North South Publishing.

A LETTER TO THE AMERICAN PEOPLE

October 5, 2016

The times that we currently find ourselves in are irrefutably chaotic. There is division all across the country, and many believe that they are being ignored by the government that was established to protect their individual rights and liberties. The country has seen troubled times before and has survived each one of them, some say stronger, but I do not believe so. Each time a country comes face to face with an impossible struggle and survives, usually, it is because of one of two reason; the people come to together united as one, or the government uses its power to force the community past whatever the obstacle is. When people join as one the country will become stronger and a better place to live, but when government power is the means to an end than a nation becomes weaker by each presumed insignificant liberty it loses to governmental oversight.

Looking back, the Civil War, the Great Depression, the Civil Rights Movement, and 9/11 were all great struggles for the American people and at the end of each one we can see a national government growing in influence and spreading its tendrils deeper into the lives of individuals and private organizations. As a community, we feel good about ourselves for making it through such hard times, but those feelings blind us to what is going on, a power grab.

From our police and civic leaders to every party that accepts a chair in the statehouse or resides in Washington, those in a position of authority are gifted an opportunity to serve the people of the nation, it is not, and was not, ever meant to be the other way around. Today we are faced with individuals at every level of government who have forgotten that fact, and those in the community are suffering for it. We must all remember that government is founded to serve the people, and when it stops being useful for that purpose, then it is up to the people to make a change.

Change will never come from an election. No matter whom you vote for in the coming weeks, they are already part of a broken system that reciprocates the whims of one party for another but never breaks with the corruption that controls it from the inside. Republican or Democrat, it does not make a difference who sits in Congress or the White House they are all party to a cycle of tainted government. Reform is the only way to fix what is broken and to give the nation an accurate representation of our social feelings.

The following treatise is not a call for revolution, but for constructive and peaceful reformation. Each word was chosen to start a discussion, and for each reader to ask questions of themselves and those they elected. The current government was founded out of such reform, and we should all remember that it is in our rights, not only as Americans, but as members of any society to demand such improvements in order to guarantee the continued securities of our liberties.

MP Murphy
Cleveland, OH

A

TREATISE

ON THE CORRUPTION OF A CONSTITUTIONAL GOVERNMENT

Introduction

"The present state of America is truly alarming to every man who is capable of reflexion."[1]

AMERICA was born with a greater opportunity for happiness than any nation before it. Her setting out in life was like an awakening for the entire world that spawned the improvement of governments across the globe. Her cause was undeniable true, just, and liberal. The conduct of her birth marked with honor, and it is not every country that can boast such origins. Any recovery of that birth, now or in the future, must depend on a return to the ideas of the founding. A project of reformation cannot be accomplished without the simple principles and experiences of its original citizens translated for a new day. Unfortunately, the mind of the nation has bowed down to the political superstition it has in the government, which forfeits a considerable portion of the powers that are necessary to make and maintain productive change. The demon that poses the greatest threat to us comes from within, and it is there that the sentinel for the republic should watch and not to distant trepidations.

---

[1] Paine, Common Sense 60,61

Society and the communion of man is a blessing in every state, but government, even in the best cases, is a necessary evil. The defects of every government, and our constitution, both on principle and form, must be open to discussion. Man did not enter into government to become worse off than he was before, nor have fewer rights granted to him than were already his by being a member of society. Government was founded to secure those rights, with a person's natural rights at the foundation of his civil rights. From these principles, the strength of government is found, and through the interest of the people, it is supported. Restraint and concern for the common good are more important than any regime or political party. Therefore, it is a much greater crime for those in government to plot against the people and their liberties, than for an individual to plot against the government.

To form a perfect government, one that would completely counteract government tendencies for corruption and abuse, to this day has exceeded the limits of human wisdom. Even governments, founded on the promising cornerstone of knowledge and perception, eventually fall to faults of man, as history has proven. In America, the constitution was established on the ideals of natural rights and *Res-Publica*, or Republic, which translates to public good. These are honest and virtuous ideals, which have public welfare first and foremost, but the tendency of all governments to pass beyond their intended limits is what exposes the liberty of a nation to danger, and is the ultimate threat to individual security.

In forming a constitutional government, it is essential to consider what are the ends to which such a government is necessary, and to execute those ends in the least expensive way. Such a task is without refute because every man wishes to pursue his dreams, enjoy the fruits of his occupation, and secure property with the least expense. Furthermore, natural rights, those that pertain to man's existence, and civil rights, those that relate to man's membership in society, need to be taken into account with relation to individual protection and security. Government only has a right to exist as a result of a compact between individuals in society. The right of people is based on their personal and sovereign rights as members of society. That is why a constitution is the property of a nation, the people, and not to those chosen to exercise the function of government.

When a government is perfect, every interest in society will be represented, but, even with the representative system, the interests of a community are often slain by ambition. A constitution only has power through the support of the nation, and the government is granted powers by that constitution. The laws created by that government may control the community as individuals, but the community has a whole, through the constitution, controls the government. Therefore, in a government that still relies on a constitution to rule, the ultimate controlling power is in the people. The people, then, must have sufficient influence to resist the power granted to the government in the constitution.

Nothing is more difficult, when forming a constitution, than equalizing the actions of government with the interests of the community. It becomes too easy for the powers granted to a government to become perverted and turn into instruments of magnified need, which are used to promote and enrich the special interest of one portion of the community over another. Therefore, it is necessary to watch against the encroachment of power and to prevent it through the restriction of individual actions inside the system. If government, with its use and abuse of authority, cannot be restricted then the community would lose its sense of liberty and the role of the population within government would be greatly diminished.

It is pertinent to render those in government responsible to those in the populace and to prevent those that rule from oppressing the ruled. It is, therefore, required that a constitution make it impossible for one interest, or a combination of interests or class, to obtain exclusive control through the abuse of power, legislation, or the courts. To keep the elected from subjugating the electors, restrictions, such as term limits and campaign financing constraints, must be set in place. Limiting power is the only weapon against the abuse of power.

A constitutional government is on one side the power of acting, and on the other, the power of preventing those actions. Power on both sides in required to secure liberty for a community. Liberty will then repay both sides through common wealth, a content population, and mutual security. However, to grant more liberty is just as deadly to a constitutional government as too much power in the hands of the elected. Balance is the key to a successful constitution, weighing individual liberties against the cost of securing liberty. When establishing the equilibrium between the powers of government against the freedom of people - natural and civil rights, the ability to pursue happiness without hindering the happiness of others, and the security of private property must all be taken into account.

Majority Rule

"Reason obeys itself; and ignorance submits to whatever is dictated to it."[2]

MAJORITY is often used in political discussions to represent the consented will of the people, founded on the reason of a numerical majority's right to rule. Most believe that the term majority applies exclusively to the numerical majority and is perceived as the only way to construct a representative government. There is a significant liability in such thought, and when building a constitutional government, that liability, will allow despotism to encroach on the rights of the community. If the numerical majority is allowed to rule long, it often becomes nothing more than the voice or opinion of the strongest interest, the most active and invested portion of the whole. Neither the majority's education or religious beliefs are strong enough to counteract the strong tendency of such rule to corrupt and debase the people it is allocated to protect. Every man is susceptible to original sin, allowing that, such inherited corruption will promote a strong predisposition for a government of a numerical majority to eventually slide into another form of absolute government.

---

[2] Paine, Rights of Man 163

Popular government or democracy, as the term implies, is a government of the people. A model for perfection in such a government would be one which could embrace the consent of every citizen under its care. However, such a mode of government would be impractical, at least to those that view the numerical majority as an accurate representation of all individuals of the community. If such a statement was true, or if the numerical majority could accurately represent the people, then our conversation would end here, as such a government would be a perfect model. The error in such thinking resides in the fact that the numerical majority does not represent the actual sense of the people because it is no more than a majority over a minority. Often the majority is not a true majority. In America, there is a large body of people who attend daily lives with no care to the everyday workings of the government. These people never come forward to share their voice, except on some important occasions. Such a reason is why the use of a numerical majority, in a representative system, does not always represent the true opinion of a country. When a significant portion of a community does not come forward and voice their views, and entrust in others that it be voiced for them, then often important issues are missed, and the results do not truly portray the feelings of the community.

The formation of a majority leads a community to be divided into two great parties, one which represents the majority and one the minority. These parties will represent a constant struggle of one group to obtain the majority, and thus control over the government, and the other to retain that control. The conflict for power, between these two groups, will be fed by the consuming of other, more individual groups, in order to maintain a constant majority. The consumption of interests will dilute the initial goals of both parties, which lead to the false representation of those individuals they claim to speak for within the government. Dilution of ideals and the struggle for the remunerations of government create a vacuum that allows for the temptation of personal power to seep in.

The biggest problem with any form of government rests in the powers that they must necessarily possess to repress violence, maintain order, protect individual property, and protect the population from outside threats. These powers cannot be executed on their own. Individuals, men and women, who, like every other individual, maintain feelings that are stronger for themselves than for the social feelings they are delegated to represent. Therefore, they cannot be entrusted with the powers invested in the government, without concern that these powers, if left unchecked, will be used to oppress the rest of the community.

There are a few instances where an individual will not fall victim to the "self," such as in a relationship between a mother and a child, but these cases are few and are becoming fewer. Modern technology has considerably developed society's obsession with the "self" and individual achievement and notoriety. Those technologies have also lessened the community's reliance on traditional values to guide them, which makes corruption of every person easier. Individuals have a greater regard for his or her happiness than for the happiness of others, whenever these two come into opposition the individual will sacrifice the interests of others for their own. When the powers of government are added to the equation, it adds for a greater need to protect the interests of the self.

By protecting one's own interests, maintaining the control of the majority, and by continuing to garner the advantages of rule; those chosen to represent the numerical majority will be nothing more than representing those interests that best keep them in position to endlessly maintain the comforts they have created for themselves through the manipulation of the system. As the country has become more wealthy and its population has grown, the difference between the rich and poor has increased bringing with it a greater tendency for conflict between the classes as the poor have become more dependent on the government. There will then, as with all numerical majorities, no want of leaders among the wealthy, those with the ambition to excite and direct the efforts of the poor, with no other purpose than to gain control over them as a means of controlling the government.

That is why, in a system of representation, everything must appear in view of the public, every man must be aware of his ownership in the government, consider it a necessary business to understand its workings, and protect the concerns of his interests instead of relying on the good nature of others. No individual within the community should adapt the unquestioning custom of following what in government we call leaders, because these leaders are in the custom of blinding the understanding of the community to make them believe government is a mysterious thing, only capable of being executed by a chosen few. These leaders are only in the business of obtaining the revenues and honors that come from their position, and human nature will not allow them to do otherwise.

Two Party System

"The tyranny of the legislature is the most formidable
dread."[3]

MISTAKES are made in supposing that the insertion of
legislation, within a constitution, is sufficient to prevent a
major party from abusing its powers. Choosing an elective
form of government will not make it less prone to abuse or
corruption as long as the weakness of man is at play. If the
elected person possesses unchecked powers, or those checks
become corrupted, then those elected become separated
from representation and begin to move towards despotism.
Furthermore, as a government grows and contains
numerous moving parts, there becomes less responsibility
among those individual parts because each part will cover
the corruption of the other. These pieces become movable
tools used to cover the mistakes or fraud of the majority that
controls them.

The conflict between two parties, the majority and minority
- over control of the government with the tributes and
rewards that come with it - will result in an array of measures
that seem best calculated to reach their end game by any

---

[3] Thomas Jefferson to James Madison, Paris, March 15, 1789

means. During such a conflict, the two parties lose focus on the wants and needs of the people they claim to represent, as it has often happened in the history of parties. Most parties end in direct contrary to the principles of their foundation. In America, both the Republican and Democratic parties now represent the opposite of their formations.

Originally nicknamed the "Party of Freedom," the Republican Party was formed by anti-slavery supporters in 1854. The "Party of Lincoln" became known for their support of the Emancipation and the Women's Rights Movement. However, during the Civil Rights Movement of the 1960s, the party philosophy began to change as they were losing ground to the Democrats under Kennedy and Johnson. The Democrats would also control Congress between 1955 and 1981. When Johnson signed the Civil Rights Act, upsetting the Democratic Party's traditional support base of White Southerners, the Republican Party began to waver on their founding principles to capture new opportunistic votes and control of the majority. Today, the Republican Party counts the White South as their sturdiest supporters, even though they were once the "Party of Lincoln."

On the other side of government is the Democratic Party, founded officially in 1828 in order to elect Andrew Jackson as president. However, the party was actually a part of the Democratic-Republicans begun as a conservative movement by Thomas Jefferson. Democratic leadership fought for small government and opposed the use of public funds for economic stimulus, which was strongly demonstrated by President Van Buren's policy during the Panic of 1837. In 1892 Democratic President Grover Cleveland won the nomination on a platform of supporting lassie faire economics, low tariffs, and supporting the continued use of the gold standard. However, a couple of economic panics, ending in the Great Depression, forced the Democrats to rethink their policies. Under Franklin D. Roosevelt the party began to abandon their old principles in order to pull the country out of the Depression, increase government departments, and provide a reason for future tax revenues. The power wielded by the government after these changes were installed, was too much to give up for the Democrats to revert to the party's founding beliefs.

Dramatic change in party philosophy is done to ensure the victory of future elections. For change within the party to take place, control is put in fewer and fewer hands, as the need becomes more desperate to enact the transformation. Changes also require party fidelity, which must be supported by rewarding partisan services. Those rewards create great zeal among members clamoring for advancement within the party structure, in order to receive increasingly superior recompenses. It is such that devotion to party becomes stronger than devotion to country or community, and the promotion of the interests of the party more central than that of the common good of the whole.

John C. Calhoun once wrote that "The struggle to obtain control of the government, elevates to power the designing, the artful, and unscrupulous, who, in their devotion to party, instead of aiming at the good of the whole, aim exclusively at securing their ascendency of party."[4] These words came from a man who was a long-term Senator and who once sat as the Vice-President. It is evident, either through his accomplishments or from those around him, Calhoun could see how party members would focus on attaining power within the party because it was reciprocated with authority in the government. Thus, members that controlled the party could, in turn, control the government if their party held the majority. By placing control of the parties in the hands of their majority, the government, under the supervision of the majority of the party in power, becomes a government of a minority over the majority.

Control of the government once passed into the hands of the leaders of the majority party, will result in a struggle to maintain a position of power against the minority party and lead to intense battles driven forward by falsehoods, slander, money, and injustice as viable weapons. The parties will attempt to appeal to all parts of society and use the lowest and most uneducated to debase and corrupt the community into forgetting sound reason in order to push forward party ascendency at a cost to principle and policy. The party

4 Calhoun, 52

battalions will further enlist human feelings to (or "intending to") promote the interest of the party at the expense of the good of the whole, which is the opposite of what government should be...a body that enlists the individual on the side of social feelings to promote the good of the whole.

The press, which should be a proponent for those social sentiments, often becomes an organ of the battle, a tool for party warfare. With its reach used by each side as a means of controlling public opinion, to promote the peculiar interests of the party, and to aid in the individual achievement of its members. As an instrument, the press contributes to party excitement when it should be exposing the faults of the system. It furthers violence and oppression by providing misdirection from actual social needs towards topics of little consequence. Money provides the means of building the mega news outlets, which control all types of media and audiences, with nothing more than personal agendas driving the message. Technology only heightens the ability of these conglomerates to lead the community astray, twenty-four hours a day.

We are now at a stage that policy and principle no longer play a significant role in the election process. The personal backbiting and indecent squabbles that candidates resort to are dishonorable to the voters and are injurious to the value placed on all future elections. Politicians born in the last century, a set of juvenile thinkers unable to see the final outcome of the picture they paint, men who go no farther with any principle than as to suit the purpose of party and self, have become so engrossed in their own self that they are no better than Narcissus gazing into a pool of water. How trifling, how ridiculous, and in reflection, how appalling do the quarrels of a few weak and self-interested men seem weighted against the securities and needs of the whole country.

Two necessary changes must be made to disengage the vicious cycle of party warfare that currently threatens the integrity of the election process and those we chose as representatives. Common sense will dictate the wisdom of having elections often and term limits installed for all those elected. With such policy, the elected will be forced to return and socialize one again with the community that nominated them. Knowing that they will be required to go back to face their electors, candidates will maintain fidelity to their community and be less tempted to build a station for themselves. The interchange, happening on a frequent basis, will promote common interest with all parts of the community, and they will naturally support each other, the elected and the electors, and create stability in the representative system.

Factions that get possession of public offices become corrupted by bribery, personal interests, and by the general benefits of those willing to compensate public officials for an ear. With extraordinary power comes extraordinary pay often in the form of campaign contributions. In 2016, the cost of a winning seat in the US Senate will reach nearly $30 million, with over $40 million being raised by the winning side.[5] These large sums leave candidates in debt to their contributors, which leaves those who do not contribute on the sidelines of forming public policy. When such large amounts of money are allotted to an individual position in government, it becomes the center which around every kind of corruption can generate and form. It further, allows the two parties, battling for power, to view the government as a profitable monopoly and the people as property of the business. To disrupt the increasing expense of running for office and the obligation of that cost, it is necessary to limit the amount associated with running for office. The current state of the election process would negate the possibility of candidates without the backing of large bankrolls from running for office, and those candidates with such resources from being exposed for corruption. A necessary step in saving the validity of the elections and the purity of the representative government would be campaign finance reform.

Some will argue that change is in the hands of the voters, but, if the system is not fixed, the minority may win the majority, but the same faults would still inflict the new party in power. There would be no change in rule only in which party was the minority and which the majority. It is in the best interest of the nation to have a thing right than to have

---

it wrong. Therefore, in a country whose government is founded on a system of election and representation, the fate of every party should be on its principles. The system of representation is the only form that can preserve liberty and embrace all varieties in a populous country. It is necessary then, to have the representation of its people real, and thus the elections real. If the elections are a farce, then the representation becomes nothing more than an illusion. High costs of running an election, and the exclusion of parties outside of the big two, keep any election from being genuine because it excludes a significant number of potential candidates the chance to run, be seen, and a large margin of people from being represented by their preferred candidate. It is not to be left to those that rule to instigate reform in the system that they benefit from, lest, it should reach them and become detrimental to their self-interest.

Wealth, War, and Taxes

"Taxes were not raised to carry on wars, but that wars were raised to carry on taxes."[6]

ONE type of government measures its prosperity by the amount of revenue it extorts, while the other proves its excellence by the small amount of taxes it requires to be productive in securing the liberties of its people. As a country grows the more diversified and extensive the pursuits of its population become. It also becomes harder to equalize the wants and needs of such a large group of people within a government, and more easy for one segment of the public to pervert its position into one of oppression and pillage over another.

Usually, the first signs of the deterioration of government are in the form of tax inequality, where, one portion of the community must pay more taxes in proportion to what it receives back in disbursements. The other portion will be allotted more disbursements than it had paid in taxes. Thus, the result is unequal fiscal actions within the government that divide the nation into two classes. One group benefits from the emoluments of government taxes, while, the other

---

[6] Paine, Rights of Man 138

bear the burden of supporting the government. However, who are the taxpayers and the tax consumers?

Such is the complexities of the American tax system that a question on taxation is not an easy one to answer. The upper class will argue that they pay the most taxes due to the fact of their higher income. The middle class will claim that they pay the most taxes because they represent the biggest portion of the population. The lowest earners will contend that they contribute the most to the government pool based on the percentage of taxes they pay compared to their income. All groups have a plausible argument, but the group that represents the largest supporter of government business is the group that pays the most in taxes while receiving the least in return.

According to the Tax Foundation[7], Americans who represent the lowest income earners, representing one-fifth of all households, receive the most in exchange for the taxes they contribute. Individuals in the lowest bracket, for every dollar they contribute, see a return on their investment of $8.21. Such a statistic should not be used to stir anger in the direction of one class over another, but, instead, to be used as a cry to examine how the government is using the revenue it collects. For instance, the middle class pays the largest percentage of taxes based on income tax alone, with the upper class paying the lowest percentage due to their

---

[7] Chamberlain, Prante and Hodge

earnings coming from capital gains and investments, where the tax percentage is significantly lower.

The question then becomes how is the government spending the revenue it collects from its citizens, and is that spending necessary? Are such generous government benefits used to enslave a large portion of the community with dependency? According to CNN, the biggest expenditures for the US fell into four categories that covered over 68% of tax money collected. These were health, military, national debt, and unemployment and labor.[8] The remaining 32% was used to cover the remaining government budget. Are these expenditures necessary? Do we need to spend eight times more on the military than we do education?[9] Finally, how does such a large tax burden lessen the liberties of a populous nation?

Another mark of oppression through taxes is the expansion of government to generate and increase the tax revenue. The effect of ever increasing taxes is to enrich and strengthen the power of those in government, while, impoverishing and weakening the community, thus, forcing them to rely more heavily on government assistance. Abject poverty equals dependence, not independence.

---

[8] Sahadi, 2016

[9] Military spending accounted for 25.4% of the budget compared to 3.6% allocated toward education in 2015 (Sahadi).

Taxes come in many forms, and most people only acknowledge sales and income tax in their daily life, but the tax burden falls heavily on the consumer in other ways. Regulation is one of the government's best forms of tax collection, with the cost of those regulations passed on from businesses to the consumer. Every time an item is purchased the consumer pays sales tax in addition to the increased price of the merchandise to cover the manufacturer's cost of production. The more regulations on the fabrication process, the higher the cost to consumers. The burden of regulation falls so heavily on the consumer that in 2009 it cost them $1.75 trillion.[10] Such taxations may prove too heavy for the laboring and productive portions of society. The crushing weight will shrink production to a point where it is no longer sufficient to provide suitably compensating jobs to the community. Therefore, more government organizations will be needed to provide support. The question lingers, are these taxes and regulations necessary? If they are, then they are advantageous. If they are not, and they require a constant apology from those elected, then the apology itself applies that they are not a needed burden on society.

Over thirteen percent of tax revenue goes to pay interest on the national debt, a debt that continues to grow every day.[11]

---

[10] Hammerton, 2011

[11] Sahadi, 2015

If the government has not gotten too large, then why does it spend more than it is capable collecting through already aggressive taxation. The people are burdened with the weight of taxes only to gamble their children's future on debt. The government system of funding is not in the money its collects or can it even be described as credit. Through legislation, the government creates on paper what it appears to borrow, and then lays out a tax plan to keep the imaginary capital in play through the interest it will pay. The imaginary capital will be sold to the nation for money already in circulation, therefore never actually creating any new currency. It is, consequently, not credit the government lives off of but the disposition of the public to pay, and to continue to pay, their taxes. However, the government's imaginary capital is quickly outweighing the amount the nation is willing to pay, which creates a discrepancy and troubling debt.

Would it not be wise, as a nation, to declare within the laws of government, that neither the legislation nor the executive has the right to accumulate more debt than may be paid during their term of office? In such a way, the country would not be saddled with the debt of its past elected, and those elected could not oppress the population with interest payments that consume a significant portion of the taxes collected.

The portion of liberty granted to the American people is just enough to happily enslave them, and is a means of collecting revenue more productive than despotism. A government so formed, can obtain more from its people then by tyranny or by a full state of freedom, which is why it is always opposed to both. However, for it to work, the people must believe that their liberties are under constant threat. That fact is why the elected are always at a readiness to participate in various wars, by constantly different motives, to procure a means of taxation. The American people have been at constant war since World War II, and the motives have changed with every episode, from dictatorship to communism and now terrorism. Whatever the excuse, Americans are led to believe that their liberties are under attack from anyone but their own government. What has become of the national clamor of terrorism, the cry from our officials that the country is in danger, and that taxes and the securities of our state must be raised to defend against it? Nothing more than death to our young men and women, the gradual imparting of more freedoms to the control of government organizations, and an economy where jobs do not equal the qualifications of the worker.

Whatever is the cause of taxation within a nation, it will become the means of revenue for the government. War becomes an excuse for taxes, and with those taxes comes additional income for those in power. Additional revenue brings with it an interest of those in government to increase power and therefore continue to seek out war. Through its productiveness, war furnishes the pretense for the necessity of taxes and the appointments of offices that bring with them great prestige and honors for those who hold those positions. The creation of new government organizations, such as the Office of Homeland Security, present new avenues to reward loyal party members, collect additional taxes to "protect the liberties" of the nation, and create greater regulations burdening commerce. No matter how much power a government has, it will never be able to prevent the insurrections and nature for war in man. Most often, we shall find that these wars and riots do not proceed from a want of more government, but that it was government that generated the cause and brought disorder to society's natural cohesion.

Conclusion

"Instead of seeking to reform the individual, the wisdom of a Nation should apply itself to reform the system."[12]

GOVERNMENT, in its simplest form, has less liability to be distorted from its original design and is easier to repair when disorder does appear. Today we find the laws of America so exceedingly complex that the nation often suffers for years without finding in which part the fault lies when something goes wrong. Some politicians will point to one part, while some point to another. Everyone is always happy to prescribe a different medication to fix the ailment, but never willing to lay blame upon themselves. Moreover, because there is rarely any urgent necessity, it is most difficult to bring those different factions together to agree upon any one line of action. Here in simplest form, lies the ultimate corruption in a constitutional system.

America has been described as a nation of laws, but laws have a tendency to be bad and good. It is safe to ponder then that a nation of good laws can be the best of all governments, a nation of bad laws the worst of all tyrannies, and perhaps America is a combination of the two…a shining example of

---

[12] Paine, Rights of Man 168

republicanism that may have fallen victim to good and bad laws throughout its lifespan. Over time the repercussions of these statutes have damaged the foundation of the constitutional system, and the mind can draw no pleasure in looking forward under the painful conviction the nation has for the present government. America is now being ruled beyond the grave by the allegiance to an illusion that we still hold the ideals of our founding. Believing that government is something does not mean it is that something, and holding principles of the past in one's heart is not the same as living by them.

History tells us that all governments fall eventually or require great reform to save their community from that failure. We can have no joy in knowing that the current government is not sufficiently lasting to ensure prosperity to future generations. Instead, we are running the generations to come into debt and oppression, so is it in our best interest to do what nature will eventually do on its own? Complete destruction is not the answer, but reform is. The outcome can only be chosen when change comes in the hands of the willing, any other way brings with it chaos, confusion, error, and fanaticism.

No society in the history of humanity has a right to make a permanent constitution or law. The earth always belongs to the living generation and to them only. Immortal power and control is not a human right and cannot be the right of any government formed by man. The present generation in

America did not make the government they are now ruled by, and therefore are not responsible for its defects, but sooner or later it will be up to them to decide if a constitutional reformation is necessary for guaranteeing posterity for the next generation.

The very founding of the American representative system is based on the ability to reform the government, as was done quietly and rationally with the current constitution. If the country ever loses sight or is blinded to that principle, then America will no longer be the land of liberty, and instead become a race of slaves to the government of our fathers. The joint effect of all the technology found in the current generation should be to increase the diffusion of knowledge and progress towards a civilization open to continued modification of its governments.

Whenever the people of a nation are well-informed, they can be entrusted with their own government, and when things get too far wrong with that government, they can be relied on to reform in the interest of the community. Education is key to a well-informed nation. It enables them to understand that preserving peace, order, and prosperity is beneficial to the whole community. It is, therefore, in the hands of the people, and not the government, which the preservation of liberty should be relied. Those that believe only through government liberty is preserved, have never thought freely on the subject, and because of this appear to agree on accepting a faulty system. There are others who see the full extent of what threatens them but hope in the end that mercy will save them. In such a line of thinking there is insanity because threats to the liberties of the community refuse the idea of justice, and without justice, there is no mercy. It is merely a trick of those seeking power.

If the pleas to the elected go unanswered, and the nation continues on its current path, the idea should be pressed to the people to convene a convention, one fairly elected, for the purpose of taking the state of the government into consideration and back into the hands of its citizens. However, knowing no matter how strongly the current may run against the state of our two-party system, policy makers would keep everything in their field of corruption and hope that only through an accident the people would achieve the changes they seek. These changes should include the topic of campaign finance, which puts campaigns and those elected in the hands of money. The ultimate cost of running for office means either only the wealthy can run or those supported by the affluent. In either case, it denotes that elections are a puppet of the moneyed and by association the government. The high cost of office also precludes those lacking funds from seeking a position in government, thus, limiting who may run for office. In 2014, thirty-seven Republicans running for the House ran unopposed, while thirty-two Democrats retained theirs seats with no opposition. That trend is only going to continue and increase.[13]

The lack of candidates with the funding to run an election also means that term limits are not needed while there is no opposition. In fact, that is why term limits for all elected and appointed government officials are necessary. If term limits are good for one part of the government, then why not all? Restricting the number of years, or times, a person can run for office decreases the possibility of their corruption. Party loyalty will also play second fiddle to community loyalty for two reasons. First, the elected must return one day to face his electors. Secondly, after the elected term ends in one position he or she may want to run for another, thus needing the positive support of their constituents. For example, a person is elected to the House after his term is up then may run for Senate, if their community so desires, and possibly someday for President. Such advancement, however, is harder than running for the same seat unopposed, and, thus, would require constant validation from supporters. Term limits do not deter a person from maintaining a life in politics, only requires them to answer more regular for their actions in office.

Lastly, an evaluation of the government organization is required. The tax burden needs to be justified, or the dismantling of large government offices need to be put in

---

[13] The Economist, 2016

place. By limiting the size of the government, the dependency on government subsidies, enforcement, and oversight will decrease. The more perfect society is; the less government is needed. The educated and productive will regulate their own affairs and govern themselves. All the great laws of human society are laws of nature. Trade and commerce, whether between individuals or nations, are laws of reciprocal interest. These laws are followed and observed because it is in the best interest of both parties, and not because of the laws government may impose. Large government is not a necessity of a populous society, and it is required for only a few cases in which society is not completely competent. If extensive government were to be abolished, society would act on its own and with common interest producing general security. There is mutual dependence within a community, and that has a greater strength than laws of government. It is the common benefit of man that holds society together like a great chain that connects us all. Every occupation, from the farmer to the manufacturer, prospers by the aid it receives from the other. Common interest, therefore, regulates their concerns and provides more security than laws and regulations of governmental institutions.

It was written that "let but a nation conceive rightly of its character, and it will be chastely just in protecting it. None ever begun with a fairer than America and none can be under a greater obligation to preserve it."[14] America's character is dependent on the continued practice of its founding principles, not its founding legislation but those principles that supported and guided the nation's birth. Every individual is born with equal rights with his human brothers, and the rights of the whole nation can be no more than the sum of those individuals that make up its community. These are rights that should never be surrendered to government, but governments naturally attempt to attack them. The rights of a person to think, publishing one's own thoughts by voice or pen. The right of free commerce, to build a business and maintain that investment without an assault through regulation and taxation. Finally, the right of personal freedom, to be whomever we want to be as long as it does not tread on the rights of others.

Let America shine, and let the world see that she can bear the burden of prosperity long into the future. We need to show that our founding virtues are as strong in a time of peace as they are in a time of war. Her reputation as a fair and just nation is as important as her independence. It is the charms of the honest, virtuous, and just that wins over the world, and forces civility from one's enemies. Dignity is the most superior power in the global arena, and it starts in the foundations of a society built on securing the rights of all citizens.

---

[14] Paine, Rights of Man 91

References

Calhoun, John C. *A Disquisition on Government*. South Bend, IN: St. Augustine Press, 2007.

Center for Responsive Politics. "Most Expensive Races." 2016. *https://www.opensecrets.org/overview/topraces.php*.

Chamberlain, Andrew, Gerald Prante and Scott Hodge. "Who Gets America's Tax Burden." March 2007. *Tax Foundation*. Digital. September 2016.

Hammerton, James. *The Hidden Cost of Regulation*. 10 June 2011. digital. 15 September 2016.

Jefferson, Thomas. "Letter from Thomas Jefferson to James Madison." *The Life and Select Writings of Thomas Jefferson*. New York, NY: Random House, 1993. 426-428. Hardback.

Paine, Thomas. "Common Sense." *Common Sense and Other Writings*. New York, NY: Barnes & Noble Books, 2005. 11-70. Paperback.

Paine, Thomas. "Rights of Man." *Common Sense and Other Writings*. New York, NY: Barnes & Noble Books, 2005. 95-254. Paperback.

Sahadi, Jeanne. *What your 2015 income tax dollars paid for*. 18 April 2016. digital. 15 September 2016.

The Economist. *How to win 99.6% of the vote*. 25 October 2014. digital. 16 September 2016.